Asana is distinctly a sign of transcending the human condition...(it) is the first concrete step taken for the purpose of abolishing the modalities of human existence. What is certain is that the motionless, hieratic position of the body imitates some other condition than the human; the yogin in the state of asana can be homologized with a plant or a sacred statue; under no circumstances can he be homologized with man qua man, who, by definition, is mobile, agitated, unrhythmic...

Mircea Eliade, *Yoga, Immortality and Freedom*

EMANUELE SCANZIANI

Metamorphosis

AN ARTIST ENVISIONS THE ASANAS OF YOGA

With text by Jennifer Abel

Garudasana

The yogi is poised in readiness like an eagle, carefully enfolding her strength in a balanced embrace as she readies herself to launch forth in flight.

THE LION

Simhasana

Simhasana conjures the energy of a lion ready to pounce, with tongue stretched out in a roar and fingers splayed wide like great feline claws.

THE CRANE

Bakasana

In *Bakasana*, the yogi envisions himself as a graceful and rounded waterfowl, extending his neck forward to graze among the reeds.

THE CAMEL

Ustrasana

The languid yet powerful neck of the camel inspires this vigorous backbend.

THE SCORPION

Vrschikasana

Despite appearances, *Vrschikasana* is neither painful nor lethal;
it is a slow and calculated balance, conjuring the strength of eight
supporting legs.

Matsyasana

Like a shocked fish snatched from the water, *Matsyasana* forces the eyes wide in awareness as the chest opens and the lower body flexes on the ground.

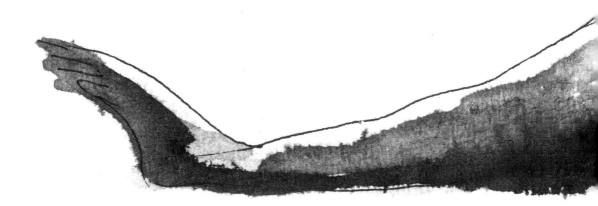

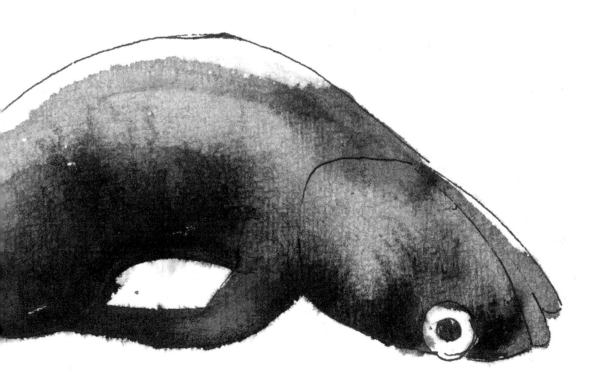

Adho Mukha Svanasana

Playful and relaxing, *Adho Mukha Svanasana* recalls the easy-going spirit of a dog just awakening from an afternoon nap.

Kurmasana

To come into *Kurmasana*, you should mimic the tortoise's unhurried pace and slink back into your shell, focusing your breath, intention and patience inwards.

THE PEACOCK
Mayurasana

In *Mayurasana*, avoid the bird's rumoured vanity and mimic instead its regal poise as the legs extend like a grand and feathered tail.

THE COBRA
Bhujangasana

Rearing up the spine gracefully, the yogi takes on the manner of a watchful cobra poised to strike. The lower body merges with the ground to support the reared head.

THE TREE

Vrksasana

In this balancing pose, the body resembles a great tree, steadfast and strong. The leg forms a deep root into the earth as the arms stretch upwards from the trunk into long, peaceful branches.

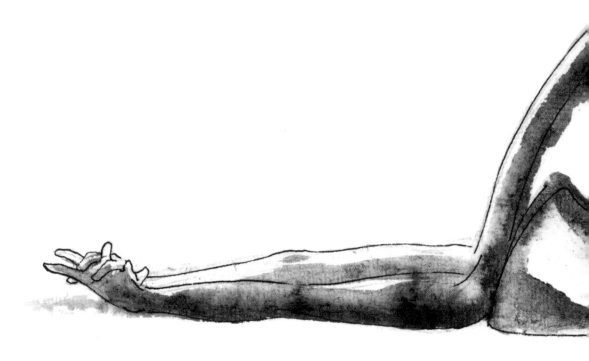

THE PLOUGH

Halasana

Essential and restorative, the graceful curve of *Halasana* sows the seeds of a nourishing yoga practice.

THE COW'S FACE
Gomukhasana

Behind a peaceful visage and drowsy eyes, *Gomukhasana* conceals a pose that demands deep concentration and physical surrender.

THE KING PIGEON

Rajakapotasana

The strut of the pigeon may seem a bit absurd, but the benefits of this challenging pose are great, as they open the hips up whilst the lower body nests firmly into the earth.

Setu Bandhasana

In *Setu Bandhasana*, the body, fixed firmly to the earth, forms a strong and steady arch from head to toe.

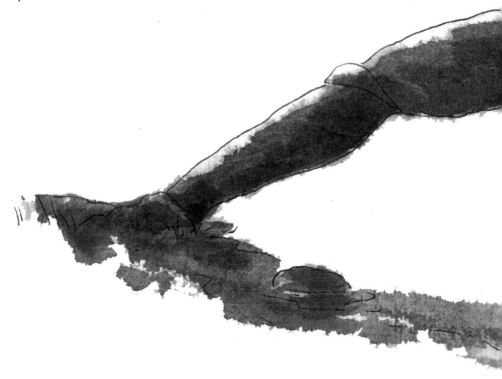

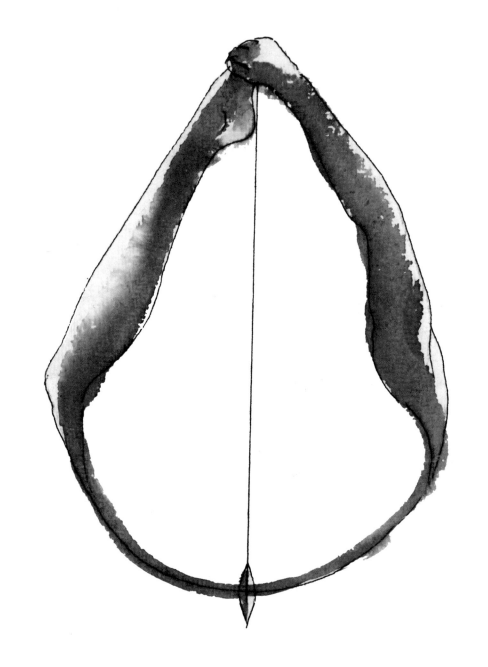

Dhanurasana

Dhanurasana honours the body's taut symmetry and strength, drawing the mind towards the abdomen like an arrow of meditative focus.

Parvatasana

Parvatasana is a meditative pose that quiets the body from base to peak, and elevates the mind into a place of still and focused contemplation.

Dhandasana

In *Dhandasana*, align your body along a single plane, allowing both strength and flexibility to co-exist within your physical architecture.

THE MONKEY

Hanumanasana

Like the mythic Hanuman, this pose requires a leap of faith in one's own body. The yogi strides over the earth towards her full physical potential.

THE WHEEL
Chakrasana

In *Chakrasana*, the yogi's body has no beginning and end, as his energy flows through him in a seamless cycle.

THE LOTUS

Padmasana

The central bloom among the yogic *asanas*, *Padmasana* relies on a deeply rooted spine to allow the mind to blossom into deep meditation.

Body,
Mind
and Imagination

Yoga can be many things. It could mean physical culture, purification techniques, breath control, or meditation. Schools of yoga are manifold and protean – and each of them swears by its own system of practice and belief. But however much the various streams of yoga differ from each other, they all agree on one point: that the physical, mental and spiritual aspects of human experience are not separate from each other, but intrinsically connected. The word yoga literally means 'yoking together', in the way a bullock is yoked to a cart. This refers not only to the connection between the physical body and the inner consciousness of an individual, but at the highest level, a union of the individual spirit with cosmic energy. So yoga is much more than just an ancient system of pilates. At the most fundamental level, it is a way of life, a disciplined striving for a more unified, focused and realised mode of existence. The paths to this goal can come from many directions.

The classic Hatha yoga tradition centres on physical practice. By assuming certain unaccustomed poses – or *asanas* – in a controlled holding, the body (and by extension one's whole being) is transformed and strengthened, as physical demands meet internal focus. The word 'Hatha' is made up of the Sanskrit syllables for 'sun' and 'moon'; and Hatha yoga simulates this union of bipolar opposites. The earliest text on yoga, the second century *Yoga Sutra* by Patanjali, maintains that when an *asana* is done with mastery, the body is untroubled by polarities. It is alert yet relaxed; at ease even in extreme positions, as body, breath and mind work in harmony.

There are innumerable schools of yoga, each with their own systemic ways of thinking about this connection. The *Yoga Sutra* does not go into the details of how *asanas* are to be practised. Later texts, such as the renowned seventeenth century *Siva Samhita*, claim that there are 84,000 *asanas*, in keeping with as many species of beings and objects. Of these, 84 *asanas* are considered standard. But there is no clear agreement on which *asanas* are fundamental and which are not. The *Gheranda Samhita* (also from the seventeenth century) doesn't distinguish too clearly between *asanas* and *mudras* or symbolic gestures. The very early texts are not specific in their descriptions of how *asanas* are to be carried out; and the various schools of yoga existing today – whether classical Hatha, Ashtanga, Bikram, Vinyasa, or Kundalini – seem to have evolved not from a single ancient text, but from more modern ones dating back to the late nineteenth century.

Their repetoire of *asanas* and variations is also from another, equally important source – repeated and tested practice. As a practical science, many yogic poses seem to have been derived from observing everyday beings and objects – birds, animals, trees, mountains, bridges or ploughs. There is a particular character to each of these beings – the sinuousness of the snake, the solidity of a bridge, the grand stillness of a mountain – which mark out their singularity. Each of them has been gifted in special ways, a manifestation of the same life force which inhabits all matter, animate and inanimate.

So in keeping with the yogic merging of philosophy and practice, the yogi doesn't just bend her body in imitation of a snake or a bridge. It is the sinuousness of the snake and the solidity of the bridge she wishes to inhabit. She stays with the pose mentally and physically, establishing a focused relationship to it. When this is strong and successful, it can induce transference, and the qualities of the object pass into her. A yogi can gain the strength of an elephant, claims the *Yoga Sutra*, through the endurance of his own concentrated thought on it.

Naming an *asana* after beings and objects in the world around us is not just a pedagogic device – it assumes that we share a physicality with the non-human and animal world which enables us to return to it. This 'return' can be seen as a communion with a world that is now distant and alienated from us, perhaps an echo of ancient shamanic practices where one wore the skin of a dead animal, or imitated the gait of a living one through dance or movement. By going beyond the body and becoming one with other creations, the yogi returns to find her own body and mind stretched, transcending its own tensility.

This is the transference that *Metamorphosis* plays with, by visualizing the body of the yogi when it meets the object of contemplation. It is an artistic celebration of the central tenet of yoga practices, capturing the moment at which physical bending and twisting merges into an inexpressible transcendence. Obviously, *Metamorphosis* is neither encyclopaedic nor faithful to any one tradition of yoga. It is also not a manual of how to perform yoga *asanas* – of which there are innumerable excellent ones available. *Metamorphosis* takes up the most suggestive *asanas* which inspired the artist, to celebrate the spirits invoked by them. This playful merging of the human form with lions, snakes, scorpions and stone bridges is a brilliant vision of yoga's potential to transform the relationship between body and mind, and in the process, celebrate the union of matter and spirit.

Gita Wolf
TARA BOOKS

Metamorphosis
Copyright © 2008 Tara Books Pvt. Ltd

Illustrations: Emanuele Scanziani
Text: Jennifer Abel
Concept: Sirish Rao & Gita Wolf
Afterword: Gita Wolf

Design: Rathna Ramanathan, m9design.com
Production: C Arumugam
Printed and bound in Thailand by Sirivatana Interprint PCL

isbn: 978-81-86211-48-9

Emanuele Scanziani would like to thank Monica Marinoni for her inspiring technical support during the posture studies.

Jennifer Abel would like to thank Diane Zantop for enriching her life with yoga.